The Hidden Mysteries
of Tao Philosophy

A GRAPHIC NOVEL

The Hidden Mysteries
of Tao Philosophy

A GRAPHIC NOVEL
BASED ON THE *TAO TE CHING*
MAY 20, 2016

By

Texts: Wayne L. Wang, Ph.D.
Graphics: Lekki Chua

王文隆　蔡烈輝

Helena Island Publisher

2016

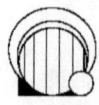

Published by
Helena Island Publisher
1717 Clemens Road
Darien, Illinois, USA 60561

Copyright © 2016 by Wayne L. Wang and Lekki Chua

All rights reserved. No part of this book may be used or reproduced in any manner whatsoever without written permission. No part of this book may be stored in a retrievable system or transmitted in any form or by any means including electronic, electrostatic, magnetic tape, mechanical, photocopying, recording, or otherwise without the prior permission in writing of the publisher.

May 20, 2016
Printed in the United States of America

ISBN   0972749675
978-0972749671

Wang, Wayne L., 1944 -
Chua, Lekki, 1936 –

The Hidden Mysteries of Tao Philosophy
by Wayne L. Wang and Lekki Chua;

(A Searching for Tao Series #6)
Includes bibliographical references

Eastern Philosophy and Religion
Cover Artwork by Lekki Chua and Wayne L. Wang

To

We dedicate this book to
Those who contribute positively to
Light Up Taiwan
May 20, 2016

and

The Whotoo Art Group Members
芝加哥胡塗畫會

Acknowledgment

We have planned to make this book a reality for about five years. It is finally possible with the support of our friends and family members. The small Whotoo Artist Group has been the invisible driving force for encouragement to complete this book.

Searching for Tao Series
尋道叢書系列

This book is part of our *Searching for Tao Series*, which deals with the nature of Tao philosophy.

1. Dynamic Tao and its Manifestations (English)
   動態的道與其顯象（2004）
2. The Logic of Tao Philosophy (English)
   道家哲學的邏輯（2013）
3. *Tao Te Ching*：An Ultimate Translation (English)
   道德經：終極翻譯（2013）
4. Searching for the Meaning of Life (Chinese)
   尋求人生的意義（2014）
5. The Logic of Tao Philosophy (Bilingual Revised Edition)
   道家哲學的邏輯 (英漢對照 修定版)（2015）
6. The Hidden Mysteries of Tao Philosophy: a Graphic Novel (English) 道家哲學的神秘：漫畫小說（2016）
7. Systems Thinking and Logic of Tao Philosophy (English)
   系統思考與道家邏輯 (2016)

Books are available at Amazon.com. English books are available as the Kindle eBooks.

Table of Contents

Introduction   1

    THE LOGIC OF TAO PHILOSOPHY 2
    SQUARE OF OPPOSITION 6
    THE STRUCTURE OF TAO LOGIC 7
    COMPLEMENTARITY OF THE OBJECTS 9
    THE PRINCIPLES OF TAO PHILOSOPHY 14
    UNUSUAL LOGIC CONSEQUENCES 18
    LAWS OF INTERACTION AND TELEOLOGY 23
    INTERPRETATION OF *TAO TE CHING* 25

References   26

Chapter 1	The Principle	29
Chapter 2	Dualism	33
Chapter 3	Upholding the Able	37
Chapter 4	The Harmonized Tao	41
Chapter 5	Straw Dogs	44
Chapter 6	Spirit of Tao	47
Chapter 7	Heaven Can Last	49
Chapter 8	No Contending	52
Chapter 9	No Overflowing	55
Chapter 10	Embracing Oneness	58
Chapter 11	Wu and Yu	62
Chapter 12	The Essence	65
Chapter 13	Favors and Disfavors	68
Chapter 14	Thread of Tao	71
Chapter 15	Ancient Masters	74
Chapter 16	Destiny	77

Chapter 17	It is just Nature	80
Chapter 18	Impaired Tao	83
Chapter 19	Basic Principle	86
Chapter 20	Yes and No	89
Chapter 21	Persistence	92
Chapter 22	Image of Tao	95
Chapter 23	Division	98
Chapter 24	Tiptoeing	101
Chapter 25	Unity of All	104
Chapter 26	Anchoring	107
Chapter 27	Without Traces	110
Chapter 28	Grand System of Tao	114
Chapter 29	Controlling Nature	117
Chapter 30	Wars	120
Chapter 31	War Victory	124
Chapter 32	Establishing a System	127
Chapter 33	Inner and Outer	130
Chapter 34	Tao Floods	133
Chapter 35	Great Image	136
Chapter 36	On Shrinking	139
Chapter 37	Self-Rectifying	142
Chapter 38	The Hierarchy	145
Chapter 39	Maintaining Oneness	149
Chapter 40	Dynamics of Tao	152

Concluding Remarks 154
About The Authors 157

Figure 1 Interaction Model 8
Figure 2 The Taiji Diagram 11
Figure 3 Patterns of Reality 13
Figure 4 Equivalence of Actions 20
Figure 5 Pattern and Objects 22

PREFACE

This is another attempt to bring our discovery of the logic of Tao philosophy to the general public. Our discussion in this book is based on the logic model of Tao philosophy, published in *The Logic of Tao Philosophy* and the translation of the *Tao Te Ching*. Some important insights are also discussed in *Systems Thinking and Logic of Tao Philosophy*. These are listed in our References.

The purpose of this graphic novel is to present the logic of Tao philosophy in a more relaxed and informal way. We shall discuss the main theme of each Chapter and use Manga conversations to highlight the principle behind in the Chapter.

The interpretations of the Chapters reflect closely the logic discussed in the References. The Principle of Tao may be expressed as the Principle of Oneness, the Principle of Complementarity, and the Principle of Equivalence. These principles repeatedly appear in all Chapters.

This volume initially contains the first forty chapters of the *Tao Te Ching* as illustrations of the principle of Tao philosophy. We may include the rest of the chapters in a later printing.

Modification Notes

We make use of Print-on-Demand (POD) technology to print this book, so we can provide continuous updates to the contents of this book. This feature is important for this book with evolving contents and new insights on this topic. The date shown below indicates the current version. The previous versions are no longer available. The copy online (www.amazon.com) is always the most up-to-date version. The revision date is shown on the copyright page.

This version is dated: May 20, 2016.

PART I
INTRODUCTION

What is Tao?

INTRODUCTION

Why is Tao such a complicated concept?

Lao-tzu did not have a school to preserve his thought, so his logic has not been explored in the historical interpretations. The *Tao Te Ching* has been subjected to unwarranted speculations. We have to recover the original Tao based on the words of Lao-tzu.

What can we do to recover the original Tao?

    This is our journey back to the original logic of Tao philosophy. Tao philosophy has become a mystery due to early, minor but critical, deviations and speculations in the interpretations. This is what we try to eradicate. Tao philosophy indeed has an interesting logic structure.

    As said by Aristotle, "The least initial deviation from the truth is multiplied later a thousand fold." Simple logical errors in the early interpretation of Tao philosophy have now become big issues between the Eastern and Western philosophies. These errors were not committed by Lao-tzu, but by early historical interpreters.

Many early interpretation errors are due to simple logical errors in what Adler (1985) classifies as the "fallacy of reductionism." This kind of logical errors is to "assign much greater reality to the parts of an organized whole than to the whole itself; or even worse, maintaining that only the ultimate component parts have reality and that the whole they constitute are mere appearances, or even illusionary." [1]

This Introduction summarizes the logic structure of Tao philosophy base on the *Tao Te Ching* itself. A full discussion can be found in the References.

The Logic of Tao Philosophy

Lao-tzu reveals the logic structure of Tao philosophy in the first chapter of the *Tao Te Ching*, and discusses how we can use dualistic language to describe a reality.

We habitually describe a reality in terms of two opposites or more appropriately, two *complements*. To describe the nature of the myriad things, Lao-tzu starts with Wu 無 and Yu 有 as two opposite ways of looking at the nature. [2] Then Lao-tzu describes how reality may be

---

[1] Adler, Mortimer J., *Ten Philosophical Mistakes*, Touchstone, Simon & Schuster,1997.

[2] There have been numerous debates on the meanings of Wu and Yu. Most of these debates are due to dualistic fallacies, and are not relevant

preserved in such dualistic thinking. Lao-tzu calls "the natural order of the myriad things" the Tao 道.

We assign various names 名 to denote the nature of the myriad things. These names represent the "parts" of the nature. These parts Wu and Yu are convenient objects that we can use to reconstruct the reality.

Real Wu and Real Yu

Since any realistic description must be a whole, Lao-tzu uses the concept of Heng 恆 to indicate undivided wholeness of Tao, as Heng Tao 恆道 and Heng Names 恆名. We do not have a convenient translation of this concept so, informally, we may simply replace *Heng* by *Real* in our discussions.[3]

Corresponding to the objects Wu and Yu, Lao-tzu designates their realistic equivalents as *Real Wu* 恆無 and *Real Yu* 恆有. The logic of Tao philosophy is the way we can use Wu and Yu to describe the corresponding realities Real Wu and Real Yu.

In our model, Wu and Yu are called the *objects* and Real Wu and Real Yu are the *actualities*. The actualities are our best representations of the reality as patterns of objects. As in systems thinking, the reality is represented by these

---

for our logic discussions. Wu and Yu could be any two opposites, and the logic structure remain the same. The logic structure is repeated in many chapters of the Tao Te Ching with many examples of different opposite pairs.

[3] This is consistent with the concept that only the whole can be real. Reality must be whole and undivided.

patterns, and not by the objects. We shall show that the actualities are *patterns* or *structures* of the objects.

Chapter One of the Tao Te Ching

Chapter one of the *Tao Te Ching* summarizes Lao-tzu's logic with a dualistic example. In a simplified view, we may first assume that the myriad things are either totally the same (Wu) or totally different (Yu). They are the same because they are parts of the same nature, and they are different because they do show differences. But in reality, the myriad things are neither totally the same nor totally different. The actual myriad things are both the same and different at the same time.

Lao-tzu very skillfully uses the following paragraphs to describe the true relationship between the myriad things. Lao-tzu says that:

- In Real Wu, we will also see the appearance of Yu. Therefore, in the Real Wu, Wu is anchored on some Yu.
- In Real Yu, we will also see that the boundaries are fading to show the appearance of Wu. Therefore, in Real Yu, Yu is anchored on some Wu.

Therefore, the reality is a mixture of Wu and Yu. One object must be anchored on its opposite in order to be real. We have to find the proper structure of the objects that can describe reality represented by Real Wu and Real Yu.

Lao-tzu further says that Real Wu and Real Yu appear at the same time and represent the same Tao. They are two equivalent ways to represent a reality.

Logical Dualism and Ontological Dualism

Therefore, we have two kinds of dualism. The objects Wu and Yu cannot represent a reality, but their actualities Real Wu and Real Yu can. Both the objects and the actualities are of dualistic nature. In order to avoid confusion, Tao philosophy distinguishes two levels of dualism.

- At the object level, we have the *traditional dualism of the objects*. The dualistic objects obey the classical logic of Aristotle. This is also known as the *logical dualism* The objects are mutually exclusive.
- At the actuality level, we have *ontological dualism* of the actualities. Since the actualities are ontological "realities," they obey a different kind of logic. The dualism is a realist dualism. [4]

In Tao philosophy, Wu and Yu are the traditional dualism and Real Wu and Real Yu are the ontological dualism. In ontological dualism, Real Wu and Real Yu are equivalent. Lao-tzu repeatedly warn against taking any dualistic object to be real, but he never denies the usefulness of these objects as our basic knowledge to communicate our thoughts on the reality.

---

[4] In traditional philosophy, it is unfortunate that the objects have been considered as real. In our model and systems thinking, these objects are are not real. Our realistic dualism refers to the ontological dualism of the actuality level.

Square of Opposition

The two kinds of dualism in Tao philosophy is similar to the doctrine of the traditional *square of opposition*, which originated with Aristotle. Here we just want to point out that the relationship between the actualities and the objects can be expressed in terms of the four corners of the square of oppositions.[5] The four corners are:

- Yu is *universal affirmative* where everything is differentiated;
- Wu is *universal negative* where nothing is differentiated;
- Real Yu is *particular affirmative* where something is differentiated;
- Real Wu is *particular negative* where something is not differentiated.

In the square, Wu and Yu are *contrary* and Real Wu and Real Yu are *subcontrary*. That is, the objects are *contrary opposites*, but the two actualities are *subcontrary opposites*. In this square, the two subcontrary opposites may both be true. This is also stated by Lao-tzu that the two actualities are equivalent representations of the same Tao.

There are many examples for such equivalence. For examples, "The cup is half full" and "The cup is half empty" are equivalent. Although "full" and "empty" are contrary

---

[5] We give a more detailed discussion in *Systems Thinking and Logic of Tao Philosophy*. See Reference 3.

opposites, but when we refer to the whole cup, the two statements are subcontrary opposites and are equivalent.

Therefore, the equivalence of Real Wu and Real Yu in Tao philosophy is consistent with this ancient square of opposition in the Western philosophy. For more details, see Reference 3.

The Structure of Tao Logic

Tao philosophy is a way to preserve reality in dualistic thinking. Chapter one of the *Tao Te Ching* starts with the traditional dualistic thinking and shows how we can preserve reality in such way of thinking. This is the logic to express the actualities in terms of the objects and:

- The objects are *simple concepts* that can be directly expressed in language.
- The actualities are *complex concepts* can be expressed in terms of the two objects.

The objects interact with each other to form certain structures as the actualities that can represent the reality. We may use the following Interaction *Model* to find the proper structure of the actuality in terms of the objects.

Such interaction model is commonly used in sciences and may be shown in the following Figure 1.

The reality is Tao. The actualities are the manifestations of Tao as Real Wu and Real Yu. The objects Wu and Yu are our basic concepts. Both levels reflect equally the same Tao. The interactions are introduced between Wu and Yu to ensure that the object level is not fragmented.

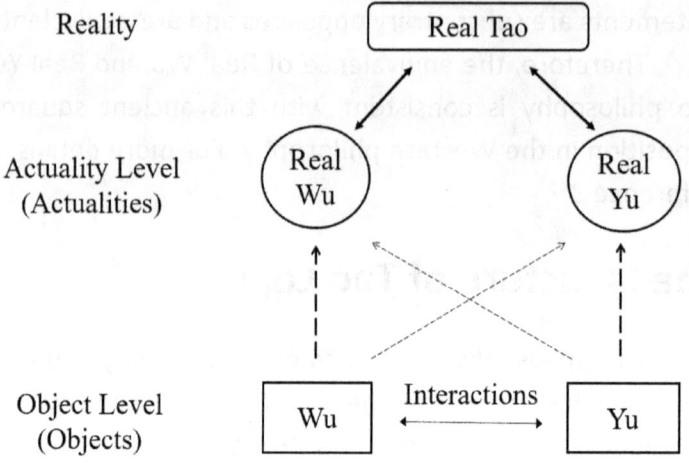

Figure 1 Interaction Model

The result of the interactions is that the objects are *superimposed* to form the patterns of actualities. The mathematical result is:

$$<\text{Real Wu}> = a <\text{Wu}> + b <\text{Yu}>$$

$$<\text{Real Yu}> = a <\text{Yu}> - b <\text{Wu}>$$

Equation 1 Patterns of Actualities

Equation 1 is the main result of our logic model. It shows that Real Wu and Real Yu consist of both objects Wu and Yu. In terms of domains, both actualities cover the same whole domain. The coefficients (a, b) are less than 1 so this equation shows that the two objects are *incomplete* and *concealed* within the actuality. In general, b is probably less than a, so an object is complemented by, or *anchored on,* its opposite within an actuality. The equation shows that the patterns of actualities have internal structures constructed in terms of incomplete and concealed objects.

Superposition is a complicate structure. The actuality is not simply a mixture of objects. The objects are *incomplete* and *concealed* within an actuality and the mixture of these objects will create *interference.* Due to such interferences, actualities will have properties that none of the objects has.

In Lao-tzu's words, the objects are rigid and strong but these characteristics will disappear or become soft and tender within the actualities. The reality is not reflected by the properties of the objects, but is reflected by the structure or patterns of the objects in the actuality.

The complete essence of the logic of Tao philosophy can be shown within Chapter One. In the following, we shall summarize the essence in terms of several principles of Tao philosophy. These principles are closely interrelated. They are all imbedded in the concept of Oneness reflected in the complementarity of the objects in Equation 1..

Complementarity of the Objects

For a realistic representation, the mathematical relations are superposition and the patterns for a realistic dualism are complementarity. Reality must be whole. Each object constitutes only a part of the whole, while each actuality is a whole by itself so it can represent the reality. The fundamental feature of reality may be expressed as the complementarity of the objects. Therefore, complementarity is the way we can use the parts to describe the whole.

In dualism, the two objects belong to two separate sub-domains, so they cannot represent the whole domain unless they are properly interconnected. A reality cannot be represented by any one object alone.

In systems thinking, all parts are interconnected. With these interactions, the two objects will complement each other to show the patterns or structure of the actuality.

Concealment and Anchoring

Equation 1 is obtained under the condition that wholeness is preserved in each actuality. Each actuality covers both sub-domains of the objects, so it is whole, independent, and free.

When we try to describe a reality with an object, the reality is complete only after its opposite object is added. This is emphasized by Lao-tzu in many chapters. If we take an object as complete, the object is no longer concealed and cannot last because it is not a reality by itself. Lao-tzu labels this object as *overflowing* 盈 and it cannot sustain by itself. If we take the two objects as two separate realities, the reality is *fragmented* 裂 and both cannot last. Therefore, the objects must be anchored on each other and concealed in patterns of complementarity.

The Taiji Diagram

The patterns of complementarity, as shown in Equation 1, has been conceptually well versed in Chinese philosophy.

Complementarity of objects may be represented by the Taiji Diagram 太極圖, as shown in Figure 2:

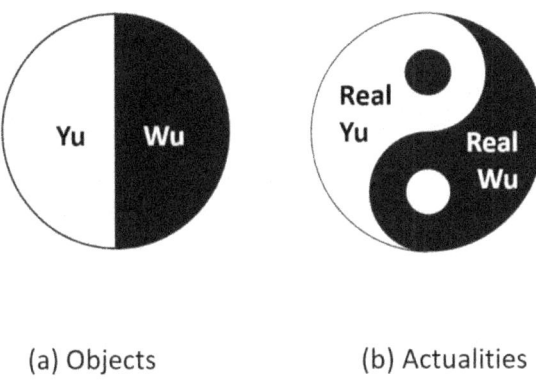

(a) Objects   (b) Actualities

Figure 2 The Taiji Diagram

The traditional dualistic objects are shown in Figure 2(a) where Wu and Yu belong to two separate sub-domains of the whole. Instead of being the opposites, Wu and Yu are complements for a whole. The *complementarities* of the opposite objects are shown in Figure 2(b), which represent exactly the actualities shown in Equation 1.

In Tao philosophy, the objects interact in the field of Chi 氣 to form the actualities. This process is governed by the laws of interactions of Tao philosophy. It is called the Te 德 in the *Tao Te Ching*.

From this, we can see that the Taiji symbol is a universal pattern for a realistic view of nature.

Harmonization, no Self-contradiction

Complementarity is based on harmonization of the objects. Harmonization is achieved by concealing the opposite objects and by anchoring one object on its opposite within the actualities.

The objects serve only as the *frame of reference* to show the actualities. The "objects" in the actualities are incomplete as objects and are not real in the whole domain. However, in our dualistic tradition, we often take the two objects as real. Since there are two opposite objects in an actuality, so the actuality will appear illusionary as "self-contradictory."

This self-contradiction is only because we think in terms of objects as though they were real. It is a common dualistic fallacy and very hard to overcome. This is a major source of difficulty in the interpretation of the *Tao Te Ching*.

At the actuality level, the contradictory characteristics of the objects should vanish due to interferences and their incompleteness. The objects are *harmonized* so the actualities are soft and tender. The interactions between the objects, in Tao philosophy, is the harmonizing Chi 氣. It is the properties of Chi that produce the original Tai-ji Diagram for yin-yang dualism.

Patterns of Reality

In systems thinking, the roles of the objects are shown in the patterns of reality.. In geometry, the two objects serve as the frames of reference (coordinates) that define a *thinking space* about the reality, or the space of the reality.

The reality in such a space requires two coordinates to represent it, so the representations are "reality vectors" in this space.

In many discussions, it is much more convenient to represent a reality in terms of patterns that can bypass the difficulty of thinking in terms of dualistic objects. Instead of superposition, we have *patterns* of objects. We may represent the actualities in Equation 1 as the pattern shown in Figure 3:

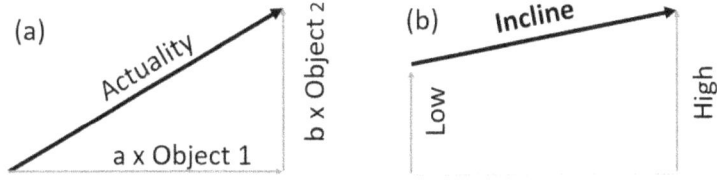

Figure 3   Patterns of Reality

Opposites vs. Complements

In this pattern representation (a), we are free from the actual meanings of the objects. Example (b) shows that two objects are used to show an incline. To represent a pattern, the two objects must appear at the same time. Our traditional thinking of the cyclic transformations between the two objects is invalid. In Tao philosophy, the general notion of Yu coming from Wu cannot be supported.

Complements vs. Opposition

In traditional dualism, we often label the two objects as *opposites* because they have conventionally opposite meanings, but in view of the logic structure, these two objects may be more appropriately called the *complements* since they complement each other to reconstruct the whole or to construct the patterns. The opposite meanings they carry have little direct significance in our discussions of reality.

To accommodate the traditional concepts, we adopt both *opposites* and *complements* in our discussions of these objects.

The Principles of Tao Philosophy

Complementarity is the foundation of all principles of Tao philosophy. The principle of Tao is Oneness. However, for our discussions, it is convenient to identify three aspects of the principle as the Principle of Oneness, the Principle of Complementarity, and the Principle of Equivalence. These three principles are closely interrelated to each other and are based on the concept of Oneness.

The Principle of Oneness

A reality must be a complete concept. In other words, a reality must have Oneness. As also stated by Parmenides that, in all our discussions of reality, Oneness must be preserved. A reality cannot be divided, but may be represented in many ways. This is the Principle of Oneness.

In dualism, opposite concepts are insufficient to describe a reality since a whole cannot be described by its parts. However, it is possible to use the objects with proper correlations to represent the reality. Because of these correlations, the objects are not independent. They form two patterns at the actuality level to represent the reality. The system may be viewed as either two interacting objects or two equivalent patterns.

- At the object level, the two objects are interconnected by their interactions as One. That is, the reality is not divided at the object level.
- At the actuality level, each actuality covers the whole domain. The condition of forming the actualities is that the actuality must be independent so it can represent the reality. In dualism, there will be two equivalent actualities to represent the same reality. So the reality, although manifests as two actualities, is not *divided* at the actuality level.

Therefore, Oneness is preserved at both the object and the actuality levels. The descriptions of the reality at the three levels are equivalent. The concept of Oneness is a universal requirement of reality at any level.[6] Oneness is preserved by the laws of interactions at the object level and by the wholeness of the actualities at the actuality level.

---

[6] The Principle of Oneness is also the core of the early Greek philosophy, the Indian philosophy, and the Buddhist philosophy. It is also observed by most modern philosophers and scientific investigations.

The Principle of Complementarity

In dualism, the realistic representations for a reality always consist of two opposite objects in complementarity.

In complementarity, the two objects are *superimposed* and will create *interferences*. Such interferences create completely different characteristics for the actualities.

The objects are concealed and only implicit within the actualities. However, we often think in terms of objects as real, so we have the illusion that the actualities exhibit self-contradictory characteristics. This is a dualistic fallacy because that we are unable to think of the whole. In order to overcome this habit, we may take these actualities as patterns of objects.

As shown in the *Logic of Tao Philosophy*, linguistic description of a reality will necessarily appear *vague, self-contradictory, and indeterminate*. Although the words of Lao-Tzu and other discussions of reality are often easily misinterpreted, the reality described is nevertheless clear, non-contradictory, and determinate, if we can understand the words with proper logic.

Complementarity is a difficult concept in a dualistic world. We may have to suspend all our dualistic judgments based on objects and convince ourselves to accept the concept of holistic patterns. We may have to rethink the nature of the two objects that we invoke to describe a reality. The two objects do not *exist* as two opposites and do not balance against each other inside the actuality.

In systems thinking, the objects are used as complements to construct the patterns that can represent the reality. They release each other from their characteristics as ordinary objects. Patterns may be represented geometrically. The two objects just define the dimensions of the reality. With two objects, the representations of the reality are two-dimensional vectors.

In modern sciences, complementarity of particle and wave, or the space and time, is very fundamental. Particle and wave are two ways to represent the classical physics. They are integrated in quantum theory. Space and time are integrated in Relativity. The concept has been discussed extensively in science and our knowledge in scientific will help in our understanding of the principle of Tao Philosophy.

In Tao philosophy, complementarity is often expressed as *concealment* and *anchoring*. A reality may be described as "mutual completion with the opposites (相反相成)." One object is often anchored on its opposite to represent a higher reality, such as "division with wholeness 曲則全," "Great Square has no corner 大方無隅", or "great accomplishment appears deficient 大器免成." We have often taken such phrases as self-contradictory, but they actually show the inherent harmony of a reality. These statements simply try to preserve the wholeness.

The Principle of Equivalence

In systems thinking, a reality is represented by two patterns (actualities), each consisting of two objects organized as a holistic pattern. The properties of the actuality are the properties of the patterns, not of the objects.[7]

The two patterns or actualities exist at the same time and are equivalent representations of the same reality. This is a paradoxical result of our model and is emphasized by Lao-tzu. The actual level is *ontological dualism*. We can also understand such a paradox in terms of the square of opposition. Under the principle of Tao, acting with Wu (Wu-wei) is equivalent to acting with Yu (Yu-wei).

Unusual Logic Consequences

There are also many unusual consequences of the equivalence principle that deserve our clarifications since they are not readily recognizable. Many paradoxical statements in the *Tao Te Ching* can become straightforward with these principles.

The opposite of a Truth is another Truth

In dualism, the two opposite objects result in equivalent truths. This is different from the *traditional dualism*, but it is logical as also shown in the *square of opposition*. The objects are contrary to each other, but the

---

[7] A familiar example in Chemistry may help us not to think of an actuality in terms of its objects. When we describe water, it is clear that we cannot think of hydrogen and oxygen. Water does not have any property of hydrogen and oxygen. The difference between water and ice is in the patterns of the objects. See Ref.1 for geometrical representation.

actualities are subcontrary so they could be both true at the same time. The opposite of a truth is another truth.

Since there is no interaction between the actualities. *Transformations* between the two actualities can happen spontaneously without any efforts. Such "transformation" is a transition between two states where all laws of interaction are the same. These changes are superficial only; there is no change in the essence since the laws of interaction do not change. The principle and the laws of interactions represented in each actuality do not change.[8]

Principle of Equivalent Actions

An actuality is a pattern of objects. It may be surprising that not only that the two actualities are equivalent, the two opposite objects are also equivalent within the principle of Tao. There is little difference in which way we start, the results are equivalent. This deserves careful consideration.

As shown in Figure 4, there are two equivalent patterns, Pattern A and Pattern B, for each reality. One pattern reflects the other pattern; the two patterns are equivalent.

---

[8] There is an interesting phenomenon in modern science called *spontaneous symmetry breaking*. A completely symmetric system may become two systems under influence of a field. However, the laws of interaction remain the same in each system.

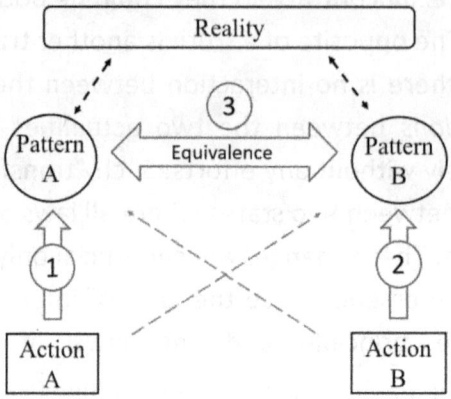

Figure 4 Equivalence of Actions

We show that the major contributions to Pattern A and Pattern B are from Action A and Action B, respectively, with some contribution from the opposite Actions. The cross contributions, shown as the dashed lines, are required by the principle of complementarity. In complementarity, Action A and Action B result in Pattern A and B respectively. Under such condition, Action A and Action B become equivalent. The condition is that the Actions are executed according to the principle of Tao.

As Lao-tzu asks in Chapter 20, "Yes and no, how much do they differ? Beauty and ugliness, how do they differ?" Our dualistic mind may fall into dualistic fallacy and consider these objects as different. But, in reality, they are not different if we follow the principle of Tao. Where and how you start is not important; the importance is the process of realization must follow the principle of Tao. The result will be the same.

Principle of Reciprocal Actions

In the same illustration, Action A, with some contribution from Action B, results in Pattern A. Pattern A is equivalent to Pattern B and Pattern B consists of Action B with some contribution from Action A. As a result, doing Action A will result in Action B. One action will end up with the results of its opposite action. In a dualistic mind, doing Action A precludes Action B to happen.

This theme is repeated in many chapters of the Tao Te Ching. For example, "Without asserting himself, he attract attention (Chapter 23)" and "By asserting himself, he will not attract attention (Chapter 24)" or "Teaching without words (Chapter 2)."

We may call this result the *Principle of Reciprocal Actions*. We have to emphasize that this is true only when everything is done according to the principle of Tao. It is actually not paradoxical; with the same goals, different actions will naturally lead to the same goal.

A Pattern must consist of All Objects

There is another common pattern in the *Tao Te Ching* worthy of some clarification. It is clear that a pattern must be constructed from all the objects. That is, Pattern A cannot be created by Action A alone by excluding Action B. This is shown in Figure 5. There must be contributions from Action A and Action B to form Pattern A.

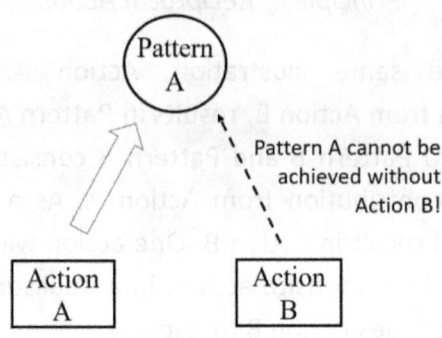

Figure 5 Pattern and Objects

In Chapter 24, Lao-tzu states: if one tries to show oneself *by excluding the action of "not showing oneself"*, then one cannot be shown clearly. The pattern cannot be built from an action alone. However, in Chapter 23, Lao-tzu states that, if one is not *just* trying to show oneself *but also include the action of "not showing oneself"*, then one is shown clearly. Chapter 23 is inclusive of all actions, so the pattern is achieved according to the principle of Tao; Chapter 24 is exclusive of other complimentary actions, so the pattern is not achieved.

In many cases in the *Tao Te Ching*, the actuality level and the object level are not clearly distinguished, so same name, such as heaven and earth, is used for object and actuality. This often create confusion. As in this example, heaven or earth cannot last as an object, but they can last as an actuality.

Introduction

Patterns are Relations

Only the patterns are real; the objects are not real. This cannot be easily understood because we always think in terms of objects.

For example, in Chapter 36 of the *Tao Te Ching*, it has been extremely difficult to understand why an expanding process could exist in a shrinking process. The reality we try to describe is a *pattern* or a natural phenomenon. Shrinking and expanding are two objects representing the phenomenon of shrinking and expanding. "Shrinking and expanding" is one pattern of the natural phenomenon.

However, if we think of patterns as the reality, then the pattern must consist of shrinking and expanding at the same time. From systems view, this is quite natural. The fundamental problem is that our dualistic mind thinks of the objects and forgets the reality under discussion.

Laws of Interaction and Teleology

The principle of Tao is maintained by the interactions between the objects. The interactions must follow certain laws of interaction in order to preserve the integrity at the object level. Lao-tzu calls these laws of interactions the *Te* 德.

The laws of Interactions

The laws of interactions ensure that the objects will result in independent actualities. This is the result of the principle of Oneness. In our formulation, the only condition we have imposed on these interactions is that the actualities must be free and independent. This is because the actualities must be realities, so they must be free and whole.

With this condition alone, we can solve the interaction model mathematically. We do not have to know the details of the interaction to find the resulting patterns. The result is that the objects will form two patterns of complementarity as the actualities. The laws of interaction preserve and reflect the Oneness of Tao.

Teleological Forces

We should also recognize that the interactions are introduced at the object level to compensate the artificial separation of the dualistic objects. Therefore, these interactions are only as real as the objects. In other words, these interactions are not real in the whole domain. These interactions do not exist at the actuality level.

The interactions are artificial at the object level. The only purpose of these interactions is to drive all objects to form actualities that can represent the reality. The laws of interaction appear whenever we are dealing with the objects in a dualistic system, from yin-yang interactions to Wu-Yu interactions. Therefore, there is a sole purpose and pattern for the interactions. Such interactions are *teleological* in nature.

Tao and Te are equivalent

In systems thinking, Tao is represented as patterns of objects and Te is the laws of interaction that support the patterns. The interactions determine the patterns and the patterns determine the interactions. So Tao and Te are equivalent.

Interpretation of *Tao Te Ching*

We have summarized in this Introduction the key characteristics of the logic of Tao philosophy. All these characteristics appear throughout the chapters of the *Tao Te Ching*. Some of these characteristics are quite intricate in our traditional views of Tao philosophy.

In Part II, we shall discuss each chapter of the *Tao Te Ching* according to the principles discussed in this Introduction.

We hope to use graphic novel to introduce this logic system in a more casual way. More formal description of the logic of Tao philosophy may be found in the References.

For each Chapter, we shall summarize the main theme and then use graphic novel dialogues to present the core principle of the Chapter. The readers will find that Lao-tzu uses many examples to re-iterate the same principle. In order to comprehend what is said by Lao-tzu, we may have to adjust our thinking habits and avoid thinking in terms of objects.

We have to think in terms of *complementarity* patterns of the objects. Systems thinking is also very helpful in viewing the patterns as the representations of reality.

REFERENCES

1. Wang, Wayne L., *The Logic of Tao Philosophy*, Helena Island Publisher, (2015). This book is translated by Mr. Ying-Tang Lu in a English-Chinese edition, Helena Island Publisher (2015).
2. Wang, Wayne L., *The Tao Te Ching: An Ultimate Translation*, Helena Island Publisher (2015)
3. Wang, Wayne L., *Systems Thinking and Logic of Tao Philosophy*, Helena Island Publisher (2016)

Part II

Interpretations of the Chapters of the *Tao Te Ching*

Chapter 1　　The Principle

　　This Chapter is fully discussed in Introduction. Lao-tzu uses two opposite objects to describe the reality of Tao. He explains how reality can be represented in dualism and describes the logic system of Tao philosophy. Tao is the proper order of nature.

　　In our dualistic mind, the myriad things have either *sameness* (Wu) or *difference* (Yu). But, in reality, they are *simultaneously* the same and different. Sameness and Difference should be in complementarity, as shown in the Tai-ji Diagram 太極圖, where the patterns of complementarity reflect the order of nature. There are two equivalent ways to represent the nature of the myriad things.

　　This complementarity pattern is valid for any two opposites. Lao-tzu has applied the same principle to many examples.

1　道、可道也,非恆道也;名、可名也,非恆名也。
2　無、名萬物之始;有、名萬物之母。
3　故恆無、欲以觀其所妙;恆有、欲以觀其所徼。
4　兩者同出,異名同謂。
5　玄之又玄,眾妙之門。

The Hidden Mysteries of Tao Philosophy

What is Tao?

Tao is the proper order of our thinking.

The myriad things look the same, but somehow they also look different.

In reality, the myriad things are both the same and also different at the same time.

How can they be both?

We have to go beyond dualistic thinking!

Interpretations of the Chapters

What is wrong with our dualistic thinking?

A reality must be a whole. Dualistic Parts are not real!

So a reality should contain both parts?

The two parts can complement each other to preserve the whole.

It looks like the Tai-ji diagram.

Yes. yin and yang complement each other in the same way.

Chapter 2   Dualism

Dualistic thinking is almost unavoidable. We always use opposite *objects* to describe a reality. The objects are co-arising and interdependent. The two objects rely on each other to have meaning. For example, in order to describe the nature of an incline, we use "high" and "low". In order to describe the nature of a task, we use "hard" and "easy."

The "opposite" ways will result in the same reality, as long as they are executed with the same principle of Tao. For example, a Sage can accomplish his task without visible action or can teach without words.

By not preferring any way, we will not deviate from the principle of Tao.

1　天下皆知美之為美，惡已。皆知善，斯不善矣。
2　故有無相生，難易相成，長短相形，高下相傾。
　　音聲相和，前後相隨，恆也。
3　是以聖人居無爲之事，行不言之教。
4　万物作而弗始。為而弗恃也，功成而弗居也。
5　夫唯弗居，是以弗去。

Whenever we think in terms of two opposite objects. We often take each object to be real. That is how we go astray.

She is beautiful!

Beautiful and ugly arise in our mind. They may be illusionary.

Beauty cannot be an illusion!

Why are they not real?

If they are objects, they cannot be real.

But they look so real.

Interpretations of the Chapters

Objects may be used to represent a reality, but they are not real.

What objects?

"High" and "low" may represent an real "Incline," but High and Low are two opposite objects.

Each object has no meaning, except with respect to its opposite.

They co-arise to show a relation.

For an "Incline," High and Low become meaningful.

They refer to the same pattern. They represent the same thing.

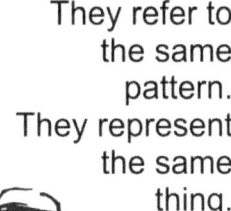

Objects become meaningful within a pattern.
Individual objects are illusionary.
In a pattern, an object is
anchored on its opposite
to become real.

Isn't that just Complementarity?
Same goal may be achieved in
two opposite ways.

If we hold on to any one explicit object,
we will lose it.

Is that why a Sage
can teach
without words?

Because he can
accomplish the same
goal in
either
way.

Chapter 3 Upholding the Able

If we do not pursue any object over others, the harmony will be maintained. Therefore, a Sage leads the people by emptying their desire for any object and building their inner strength as a whole. If we maintain the wholeness of nature, then everything will self-manage in harmony.

When we let any object become explicit, then both objects are explicit and nature becomes fragmented and will be in conflict. For example, when wealth becomes an object of persuit, then its opposite, thievery, will also appear.

Tao is to guide people in harmony with the whole. People will not pursue the differences and act with fragmented knowledge. Then we can keep all things self-managed within the whole.

1 不尚賢，使民不爭；不貴難得之貨，使民不為盜；
　不見可欲，使民不亂。
2 是以聖人之治：虛其心，實其腹，弱其志，強其骨。
3 恆使民無知、無欲也。使夫智不敢，弗為而已。
4 則無不治矣。

The Hidden Mysteries of Tao Philosophy

By taking a particular ability as an object to pursue...

People will chase after the objects in chaos.

When treasure is accumulated, thieves will appear after it.

They co-arise: treasure and thief!

If treasure remains concealed in harmony ...

Then there is no thief! Because no object to chase after.

Interpretations of the Chapters

| With inner wholeness, everything will be in harmony! | Then everything will be in its proper place! |

Nothing will be left un-managed!

He teaches people to have wisdom of wholeness without acting with fragmented knowledge, to rid of their desires for objects.

Chapter 4 The Harmonized Tao

Tao remains so vast and has served as the source of the myriad things. We can designate various myriad things from nature. Tao always looks empty of objects, but we create various objects out of this emptiness. Nature is in harmony.

Lao-tzu describes the nature as all sharpness dulled, all entanglements unraveled, all brightness harmonized, and all dust homogenized. Tao is almost imperceptible.

We do not know the origin of nature. It exists prior to appearance of any primordial images.

1 道沖，而用之又弗盈也。淵呵似萬物之宗。
2 挫其銳，解其紛；和其光，同其塵；
3 湛呵似或存。
4 吾不知其誰之子，象帝之先。

The Hidden Mysteries of Tao Philosophy

Tao always looks empty, but we can extract the myriad things from it.

Who creates everything from it?

We create everything. Everything should remain harmonized within the whole.

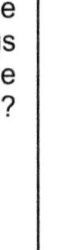

How can we treat the myriad things we have created?

That is exactly what Lao-tzu tries to tell us!

We should dull the their sharpness. We should unravel their complexity.	We should harmonize their brightness. We should blend them with their environment. 
Everything becomes imperceptible! 	But everything is there. 
We return to the primordial state of nature. Where is this Tao from? 	Tao has been there well before we designate any image of the myriad things! 

Chapter 5   Straw Dogs

Nature is free from any dualistic preference, such as benevolence or non-benevolence. The myriad things have their natural courses. Everything has a divine purpose as though a straw dog. It is holy on the altar, but after serving its purpose, it is discarded without any hesitation.

All things appear and disappear in a natural process. Lao-tzu says that nature is like a bellows. All things move in and out of it with no differentiation.

We cannot understand this process by reasoning; we just have to accept the nature as it is. We should remain neutral and hold no preference and let nature run its course.

1　天地不仁，以萬物為芻狗；
　　聖人不仁，以百姓為芻狗。
2　天地之間，其猶橐籥與！
　　虛而不屈，動而愈出。
3　多聞數窮，不若守於中。

The Hidden Mysteries of Tao Philosophy

We come and go to serve a purpose?

Why nature moves like a bellows?

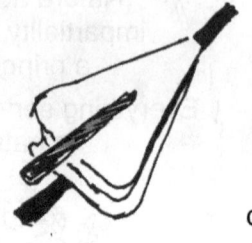

It never collapses.

Everything moves in and out, with no preference.

It keeps yielding more.

That's the way nature is. It is beyond any reasoning. There is a hidden principle.

We just have to live with the principle.

Chapter 6   Spirit of Tao

The spirit of Tao is everlasting and serves as the mysterious source of the myriad things. This source seems imperceptible but is inexhaustible.

The Spirit and God never cease.[9] We take these manifestations as the base to form the myriad things in our mind. These manifestations are the primordial source for all things (玄牝).

Tao's manifestations are forever existing and there is no end to its function as the source for the myriad things.

1   谷神不死，是謂玄牝。
2   玄牝之門，是謂天地根。
3   綿綿若存，用之不勤。

---

[9] Lao-tzu in Chapter 60 describes the holistic manifestations of Tao in the phenomenal world as two things: the *explicit* manifestation is called "God 神", and the implicit manifestation is called "Spirit 靈 (or Ghost 鬼)." In Chinese, the word for Ghost is synonym with the word for valley 谷.

Tao manifests as God and Spirit. They are always there. From this source, we form the myriad things.

It is the order of the world!

Then it is the root of everything. Heaven and earth.

The order seems ceaseless and perceptible.

Tao remains hidden?

But, it works effortlessly.

Chapter 7　Heaven Can Last

Heaven and earth can endure forever, because they do not exist separately. Heaven and earth are two objects that make up the nature as a whole, they complement each other so they can last forever together as a whole. Heaven as an object cannot last, but heaven as an actuality can last forever. An everlasting heaven must be formed by heaven as an object together with its complement (earth as an object).

In our principle of equivalent actions, one action will lead to the same result that can be achieved with its opposite action. Lao-tzu describes that when a Sage withdraws from the front, he will appear to be leading in the front. A Sage foregoes himself, so he can endure. When we act without our Self, we can accomplish what we want for our Self.

1　天長地久。
　　天地所以能長且久者，
　　以其不自生，故能長生。
2　是以聖人退其身而身先，外其身而身存。
3　非以其無私邪？故能成其私。

Heaven and earth can last long, become they complement each other.

They do not exist individually by themselves.

How can they last forever?

When you are not trying to sustain yourself, you can forever sustain.

Yes. you achieve through complementarity.

Interpretations of the Chapters

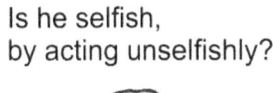

In fact, a Sage is neither selfish nor unselfish, he only performs according to the principle of Tao.

Chapter 8   No Contending

We should be in harmony with our environments, so we can contribute and benefit harmoniously to the environment.

We have to be skillful, effective, or beneficial (i.e., 善) in dealing with our environments. This is the way of Tao. The best example is water, which benefits everything in its environments and remains tranquil. It adapts to anywhere, even the places disliked by all others.

Therefore, wherever we live, we should adapt to the environment and benefit the place. We should keep our mind vast for all the things around us; we should show our benevolence to all; we should speak with trustworthiness; we, should eradicate with justice; we should act with our ability and with good timing.

The key is not to compete against whatever we have encountered as nature. By doing so, there will be no resentment from our environment.

1　上善若水。水善利萬物而又靜。
　　居眾人之所惡，故幾於道。
2　居善地，心善淵，與善仁，言善信，正善治，
　　事善能，動善時。
3　夫唯不爭，故無尤。

Interpretations of the Chapters

Chapter 9   No Overflowing

All things must be concealed in wholeness. Anything that is not concealed will not last. All objects in harmony should not emerge from the whole.

If we force an object to emerge from the whole, it will not last and then harmony is then fragmented. There is no exception.

For example, if we sharpen by excessive whetting, then the sharpness cannot be preserved. If wealth is accumulated and visible, it cannot be protected from thievery. If any grandiose is proudly displayed, it will invite misfortune.

The way of heaven is not to dwell on a task when harmony is achieved.

1　持而盈之，不若其已。
2　揣而銳之，不可長保。
3　金玉滿堂，莫之能守。
4　富貴而驕，自遺其咎。
5　功遂身退，天之道也。

Pursuing an object exclusively will fragment the whole of nature.

Maintaining harmony is the goal.

I am trying to make it perfect!

Your perfection may be unnatural. Let it be!

This is extremely sharp!

But, it cannot be preserved!

       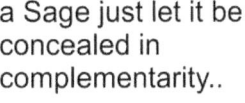 

Chapter 10   Embracing Oneness

The principle of Tao is to maintain Oneness for all.

Can we embrace all dualistic things, such as body and soul, into One? Can we conceal all objects and make them soft and tender via harmonious Chi 氣? When we encounter the myriad things, can we see them clearly without dust on our window to the world (玄鑒)?

Can we govern a kingdom without relying on fragmented knowledge? Can we keep our senses and knowledge in submissive state? Can we recognize that even extensive knowledge is not wisdom?

Embracing Oneness is to return to the natural state, where we help things spread and grow, without controlling them. Can we act without bias? The principle of Tao is to let all things be in One.

1 載營魄抱一，能毋離乎？摶氣致柔，能嬰兒乎？
   滌除玄鑒，能毋有疵乎？
2 愛民治國，能無以智乎？天門啟闔，能為雌乎？
   明白四達，能毋以知乎？
3 生而弗有也，為而弗恃也，長而弗宰也，
   是謂玄德。

Interpretations of the Chapters

Te is the way to preserve the order of nature. This order is Oneness. All myriad things should maintain their reality within the One.

In a dualistic world, how can we embrace Oneness?

Just keep all objects in complementarity.

The Hidden Mysteries of Tao Philosophy

How can we embrace body and soul as One?

They complement each other as unseparated two, as one.

How do we harmonize the Chi?

The objects are harmonized by Chi to become as soft and tender as an infant.

Objects are like dust on the mirror.

They block our view to the world. We often could not see clearly.

Interpretations of the Chapters

How about Oneness in our daily affairs?

Managing a country?

Use wisdom, not knowledge. knowledge is fragmented.

We see so many things. How can we avoid the objects?

It is very hard. Just keep them subduced.

Objects block our views.

What we know are not wisdom. The wisdom recognizes all things without differentiation, acts without preference, and support without controlling.

Chapter 11   Wu and Yu

This Chapter shows the examples of complementary.[10]

When thirty spokes fit onto a wheel, the function of the wagon is supported by both the spokes (Yu) and the empty hub (Wu) together. In systems views, the pairs of objects form a pattern that represent the function of the system. When we treat "Wu and Yu" as a complementary pair, this chapter can be interpreted consistently and naturally.

What makes a cart possible is the complementarity of the hub (Wu) and the spokes (Yu). The hub is not more important than the spokes. This is a very import shift from the traditional interpretation.

1　卅輻共一轂，當其無有，車之用也。
2　埏埴而為器，當其無有，器之用也。
3　鑿戶牖，當其無有，室之用也。
4　故有之以為利，無之以為用。

---

[10] The traditional Tao philosophy often adopt "Yu comes from Wu" as a cornerstone of Tao philosophy. This makes this Chapter very awkward to interpret. This is a clear logical error. Our model supports the co-arising of Wu and Yu.

Interpretations of the Chapters

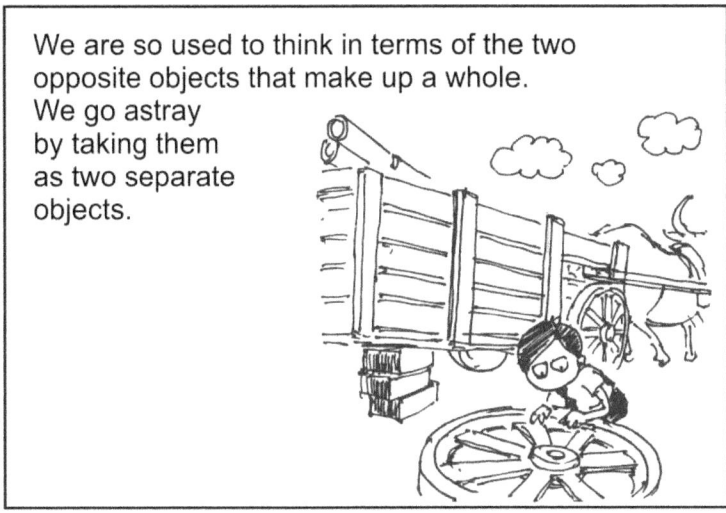

We are so used to think in terms of the two opposite objects that make up a whole.
We go astray by taking them as two separate objects.

This chapter has never been properly interpreted. Our logic model provides a natural interpretation. The same principle applies to any pair of objects that make up a whole.

A wagon can function only if the spokes and the hub complement each other.

They together support a function!

The Hidden Mysteries of Tao Philosophy

The spokes and the hub are equally important.

The hub is not more important than the spokes, or vise versa.

They must complement each other.

The two objects must be always together.

So, they can support each other.

The spokes form the shape of the wheel.

The hub allows the wheel to turn.

Chapter 12   The Essence

If we fall into the object level, then we have to deal with explicit objects and their interactions. We often pursue objects and lose harmony of the whole.

We are often deluded by our senses of sights, sounds, and tastes. We become blind of the reality behind these objects. We are pre-occupied with the objects and become numb to the delight of the whole. Pursuing these objects or accumulating such objects will hinder our path to live with the whole. Therefore, the Sage advises us to build inner strength and ignore such superficial objects.

The inner strength is to seek the essence of the whole and to maintain the whole. This is according to the principle of Tao to keep all objects concealed in harmony.

1　五色令人目盲，五音令人耳聾，五味令人口爽。
2　馳騁田獵，使人心發狂。難得之貨，使人之行妨。
3　是以聖人之治也，為腹不為目。
4　故去彼而取此。

Various senses often detract our mind from the whole. We often become overwhelmed by the things in the world.

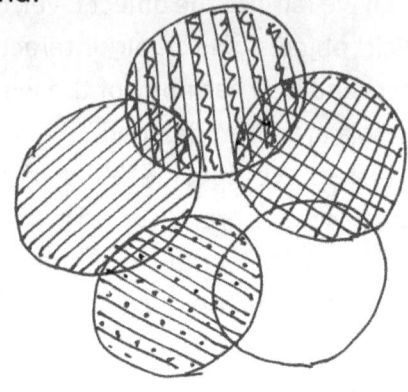

We blindly chase after the objects...

Many are mad chasing in the field !

Many objects often distract us from the path to search for the principle of Tao.

Interpretations of the Chapters

What is the better way!

Of course, a Sage will choose a different way.

How?

The sage relies on the inner strength to seek the harmony of the whole.

A sage will choose to follow Tao, instead of chasing superficial objects.

Chapter 13   Favors and Disfavors

When we separate ourselves out of the world, we will constantly experience favors and disfavors. If we are in harmony with the world and will be free from such actions.

We often falsely treat our Self as real. If we treat ourselves and the world as a whole, then these favors and disfavors will lose their characteristics and our interactions with the world will not create any distress. The interactions become the harmonizing forces and Self and the World become complementary. There will be harmony:

- We can trust the world since we are part of the world;
- The world can rely on us since the world is part of us.

These are the true states of the Self and the world.

1　寵辱若驚，貴大患若身。
2　何謂寵辱若驚？寵之為下。
　　得之若驚，失之若驚，是謂寵辱若驚。
3　何謂貴大患若身？吾所以有大患者，為吾有身也。
　　及吾無身，吾有何患？
4　故貴為身於為天下，若可以託天下矣；
　　愛以身為天下，如可寄天下矣。

Interpretations of the Chapters

How should we deal with favors or disfavors in our lives?

We often treat favors and disfavors as something for or against us.

I love favors and hate disfavors.

We become concerned if we get any disfavor.

I feel good when I am favored.

The Hidden Mysteries of Tao Philosophy

Why do we feel that way?

Because we separate Self from the world.

Isn't the world external to us?

When we are separated form the world ...

We feel every change in the world.

We become anxious.

When we are one with the world, we can entrust ourselves to the world, and the world can be entrusted to us.

There is no favor or disfavor.

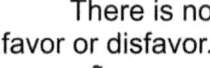

Chapter 14   Thread of Tao

Tao is invisible, inaudible and imperceptible. It is formless and objectless. We cannot describe Tao with our senses. All our descriptions are inadequate. We have to return to the state of Oneness.

Oneness has perfect symmetry. We cannot distinguish between up and down, light and dark. It cannot be described as a thing, so it seems empty of things. Oneness seems a form that is formless; its image seems nothing and seems fleeting. With perfect symmetry, there is no face and no tail.

The principle never changes. From how Tao manages today's affairs, we can see how Tao manages all since its ancient beginning. There is an unbroken *Thread of Tao*. This thread of Tao remains forever the same, independent of time and space.

1   視之而弗見，名之曰微；聽之而弗聞，名之曰希；昏之而弗得，名之曰夷。
2   三者不可致詰，故混而為一。
3   一者，其上不皦，其下不昧。繩繩不可名也，復歸於無物。
4   是謂無狀之狀，無物之象，是謂惚恍。
5   隨之不見其後；迎之不見其首。
6   執今之道，以御今之有，以知古始。
7   是謂道紀。

Interpretations of the Chapters

Its top is not bright; its bottom is not dark. It is invisible and returns to nothingness. 	It is a formless form, and is an object-less object. 
From behind, we cannot see the back; From front, we cannot see the face. 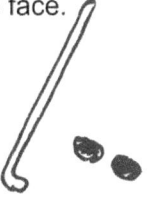	Is Tao always so? 
The ancient principle is still reflected in the affairs of today. 	There is an unbroken thread of Tao. 

Chapter 15 Ancient Masters

A master of Tao is always concealed in his environment and appears to be well beyond our comprehension. We can only reluctantly describe him in some way. He does not exhibit any definite characteristics. All things about him look uncertain and chaotic, but he seems solemn like a vast valley with tranquility. He seems to be in the state of Simplicity (Pu).

However, he adheres to a principle. Despite his unclear appearance, he can actually induce clarity around him; despite his stagnant appearance, he can actually move everything to life around him.

He chooses to remain concealed. Anything emerging from a whole will lead to an end and will be against the principle of Tao.

1 古之善為道者，微妙玄達，深不可識。
2 夫唯不可識，故強為之容：
3 曰豫焉若冬涉水；
4 猶呵其若畏四鄰；儼呵其若客；
   渙呵其若淩釋；敦呵其若樸。
5 混呵其若濁；曠呵其若谷。
   濁而靜之徐清；安以動之徐生。
6 保此道不欲盈。是以能蔽而不成。

Interpretations of the Chapters

What does a master of Tao look like?

His characters are subtle, obscure, and beyond comprehension.

Because he is One with nature.

With great simplicity, he is ready to vanish.

He looks uncertain!

He looks like a sincere guest in his neighbor.

The Hidden Mysteries of Tao Philosophy

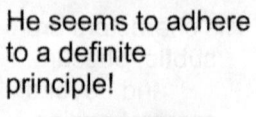

Chapter 16   Destiny

Everything has a destiny. The nature seems empty and in genuine tranquility. However, in it, we can observe the recurrences of the myriad things flourishing. The myriad things seems to have a common root, a common destiny, and a normal path. There is an unchanging order. All things remain tranquil and follow an order.

Lao-Tzu says, if we can follow this order, we will be able to appreciate the process. If we are unable to follow the order, we will run into mishaps. Knowing this order, we will become more receptive and impartial to all natural events.

When everything remains concealed in this process, there will be no danger.

1　致虛極也，守靜篤也。萬物並作，吾以觀其復也。
2　夫物芸芸，各復歸其根。歸根曰靜。靜，是謂復命，復命常也。
3　知常明也。不知常，妄。妄作，凶。
4　知常容，容乃公，公乃王，王乃天，天乃道，道乃久。
5　沒身不殆 。

In extreme emptiness and in
the true tranquility, the myriad things flourish.
We observe such recurrences.

The myriad things flourish naturally. They are anchored to their roots.

Anchored to the roots, they are tranquil. They reconcile with their destiny.

Interpretations of the Chapters

This is the norm. If we follow this norm, we are enlightened.

If we do not follow this norm, there will be mishaps.

From this norm, we become more inclusive and more unified. We become more receptive of the laws of heaven, closer to Tao and can last forever.

Isn't that the way of Tao?

Yes! Everything follows the norm.

We can be free from disasters.

Chapter 17   It is just Nature

Although nature seldom articulates its purpose, we should have faith in nature.

When we are one with nature, we are not even aware that nature exists. When we start to be aware of nature as our environment, we may praise it and want to reconnect with it. When we start to see nature as an external thing, we may feel the forces from the nature and become afraid of nature. At worse, nature becomes something we do not like.

These show our various degrees of trust with our environment. When we have enough faith in the nature, we can trust the world and integrate fully with it. If we lose faith in nature, we start to deviate from nature and eventually become distrust of the nature.

Nature appears leisurely and seldom explains how it works. It accomplishes its work and remains concealed. When all things are done, people will say that is just nature.

1 太上，下知有之；
   其次，親譽之；
   其次，畏之；
   其下，侮之。
2 信不足，安有不信。
3 悠呵其貴言也。
4 成功遂事。
   而百姓皆謂我自然。

The order of nature is everywhere.

Sometimes, we just follow it;
Sometimes, we love and praise it;
Sometimes, we are afraid of it;
Sometimes, we despite.

Why do we feel so differently?

It shows our trust in nature. When we lack faith in nature, we will be unable to trust the nature.

It all depends on us. Nature never changes.

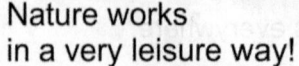

Nature works in a very leisure way! 	It just accomplishes all its work. 
When everything is done naturally... 	We say: It is just nature. 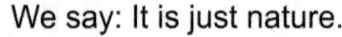

Chapter 18   Impaired Tao

When we are with Tao, everything remains concealed. When the great Tao is fragmented, we have to rely on the explicit interactions between the objects to maintain harmony.

When we are in harmony with Tao, there is no explicit rule. There is a hierarchy of integration with Tao. Lao-tzu gives four examples here.

When the Great Tao is in ruin, we have to rely on the next level of Ren (Benevolence) 仁 and Yi Righteousness) 義. When family rivalry is rampart, we will see explicit demands for filial piety and compassion. When we have to rely on fragmented knowledge, there will be unresolvable deceptions. When a country is in turmoil, there will be some royal ministers.

The general rule is that, whenever one level cannot be maintained, we have to resort to the lower level to recover. The principle of Tao is applicable at all levels.

1   故大道廢，安有仁義。
2   六親不和，安有孝慈。
3   智慧出，安有大偽。
4   邦家昏亂，安有貞臣。

The Hidden Mysteries of Tao Philosophy

When we are not one with Tao, we are look for rules of Tao.

When we deviate from Tao, the rules of Tao appear.

When we deviate from Tao, what happens?

We see the explicit rules of Ren and Yi. We try to recover Tao.

Interpretations of the Chapters

When family rivalry is rampant ... We talk about filial piety and family compassion..

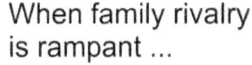
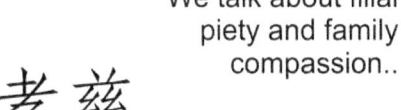

When a country is in turmoil ... We can truly identify loyal ministers.

When we do not maintain our wisdom and rely on fragmented knowledge. Then we may encounter great deceptions.

Chapter 19   Basic Principle

What is the fundamental principle of Tao?

If we can overcome the fragmented knowledge and the endless debates, people will benefit a lot. We can go beyond knowledge, beyond deception, beyond cunningness to benefit people, to restore filial piety, and to rid of thievery.

But these are only examples. There is an important fundamental principle behind all these examples.

The basic principle of Tao is: we should hold on to the simplicity of Tao by subduing our selfish desires and by reducing our sense of Self. If we can follow this principle, we can learn the way of Tao without any anxiety.

1　絕智棄辯，民利百倍。
　　絕偽棄詐，民復孝慈。
　　絕巧棄利，盜賊無有。
2　此三言也以為文，未足。
3　故令之有所屬：見素抱樸，少私而寡欲。
4　絕學無憂。

Interpretations of the Chapters

Tao is beyond knowledge, deceptions, and cunningness.

People will benefit if we avoid fragmented knowledge ...	People will to filial piety if we avoid deceptions ...	People will not be cunning if we avoid shrewdness...

The Hidden Mysteries of Tao Philosophy

There is a fundamental principle behind all these.

What is the fundamental principle of Tao?

How can people benefit more?

We can just return to the state of Simplicity by diminishing our selfness and subduing our desires.

We should just follow the principle of Tao!

If we follow this principle, the ultimate learning can be achieved without anxiety.

Chapter 20   Yes and No

When we choose two ways to look at a reality, how much do they really differ? Some people are pre-occupied with objects, while some appear indifferent to the objects.

Some cling to the objects as though they were real and the master of Tao may choose to stay with the whole and let objects appear and disappear in front of him. He never holds on to any. He looks different from other people because he keeps close to the principle of Tao as the nourishing source.

Are the masters and common people really that different? This chapter may indicate that we may choose different ways to live, but it is not really that different. [11]

1　唯之與呵，其相去幾何？美與惡，其相去何若？
　　人之所畏，亦不可以不畏人。荒呵，其未央哉！
2　眾人熙熙，如享太牢，如春登臺。我泊焉未兆，如嬰兒未咳；
　　儽呵，似無所歸。
3　眾人皆有餘，我獨遺。我愚人之心也！沌沌呵。
4　俗人昭昭，我獨若昏呵。俗人察察，我獨悶悶呵。
5　忽呵，其若海，恍呵，若無所止。
6　眾人皆有以，我獨頑以鄙。
　　我欲獨異於人，而貴食母。

---

[11] This is hard to envision, but as long as they live by the principle of Tao, they may not be that different. See *Principle of Equivalent Actions* in the Introduction for details.

The Hidden Mysteries of Tao Philosophy

We always think in terms of two opposites.

If one is right, the other must be wrong.

Are they really that different? I have chosen a simple way to live.

Your life look very different. Most people pursue a busy life.

I rather remain without any goals and anchor to nothing.

You look like a fool!

Others show abundance, but I abandon all.

Chapter 21   Persistence

Nature is a system of dynamic process. The nature does not stay at a state forever. It rains and the wind blows. Rain or wind cannot last forever. As a man, we also cannot stay in a state all the time. Nature shows many states; man must also adapt to various states.

When we are with Tao, our actions behave with Te which is implicit. When we deviate from Tao, we are lost and have to deal with explicit things and their interrelations. In these lost states, the principle of Tao becomes explicit and the rules become more complicated.

However, we are still guided by the same principle of Tao. It appears in different forms.

1　希言自然。
2　飄風不終朝，暴雨不終日。孰為此。
3　天地而弗能久，而況於人乎？
4　故從事而道者同於道；德者同於德；失者同於失。
5　同於德者，道亦德之；同於失者，道亦失之。

Interpretations of the Chapters

Even nature cannot sustain forever! How can a man?
What should we do in this changing world?

Nature is dynamic. 	We also have ups and downs. 	How to maintain our sanity? 
Nature looks chaotic when we try to hold on. 		How should we look at nature then? 

The Hidden Mysteries of Tao Philosophy

When we are in complete harmony with Tao, everything is implicit. We just follow Tao unconsciously.

We are not even aware of Tao!

What if we are not with Tao?

We have to consciously follow the principle of Tao. That is what Lao-tzu calls the Te 德!

Sometimes we are lost.

When we are lost, more explicit rules will appear to guide us to restore to the state of Tao.

Chapter 22   Image of Tao

The Grand Te 孔德 reflects exactly the image of Tao. It is the principle of Tao.

When we view nature (Tao) in terms of objects, the objects will appear to be fleeting. The objects may appear and disappear randomly. In its short appearances, Tao seems to show some object; in its short disappearances, Tao seems to show some image. Although Tao remains imperceptible and concealed, it is authentic, with essence, and trustworthy.

Since the ancient time, such manifestations of Tao never cease. This is the way we will know the nature of Tao.

1　孔德之容，惟道是從。
2　道之物，唯恍唯惚。
　　惚呵恍呵，中有象呵。
　　恍呵惚呵，中有物呵。
3　窈呵冥呵，其中有情（精）呵。其情甚真，其中有信。
4　自今及古，其名不去，以順眾父。
5　吾何以知眾父之然，以此。

The Hidden Mysteries of Tao Philosophy

Tao is the order of nature;
Te is the principle of Tao.
Te reflects exactly Tao.

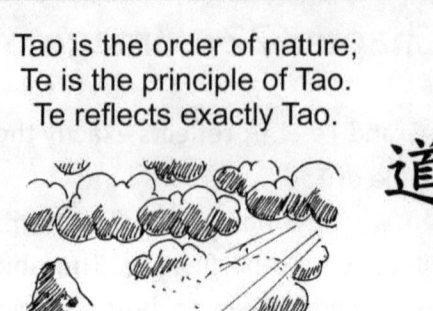

In nature, we perceive myriad things fleeting in harmony.

They follow the Grand Te 孔德.

We try to hold on, so they appear fleeting.

Tao is not fleeting. A reality is never fleeting.

Interpretations of the Chapters

Tao is imperceptible as a thing, but its essence is always there!

Sometimes, it has image; sometimes, it appears like an object.

The essence is there.
It is true and trustworthy.

Tao has been here since the ancient time.
It remains always the same way.

But, everything is changing!

Things may change, but the principle remains the same!

Chapter 23   Division

When we think of a thing, we also have to think of its opposite (complement) so the whole is not fragmented.

For example, when we divide, we have to preserve the *wholeness* in the divided "parts." Our common error is to treat each "part" as a separate reality. A Sage chooses Oneness as the guidance for all thinking.

The opposite actions will lead to the same reality if they are executed according to the principle of Tao. This is a subtle point in the logic of Tao philosophy. One action may achieve the results of its opposite action.[12]

For examples, we can achieve distinction by not showing our distinction. When we do not boast about our own merits, we gain more merit. These statements seem to be paradoxical, but they are true logically.

1　曲則全，枉則直；窪則盈，敝則新；少則得，多則惑。
2　是以聖人執一，以為天下牧。
3　不自見故明；不自是故彰；不自伐故有功；弗矜故能長。
4　夫唯不爭，故莫能與之爭。
5　古之所謂曲全者，豈虛語哉！誠全而歸之。

---

[12] See the principle of equivalent actions in the Introduction.

Interpretations of the Chapters

The principle of Tao is Oneness.
All things should be complementary.

When we divide, we have to maintain the whole.
Why and how?

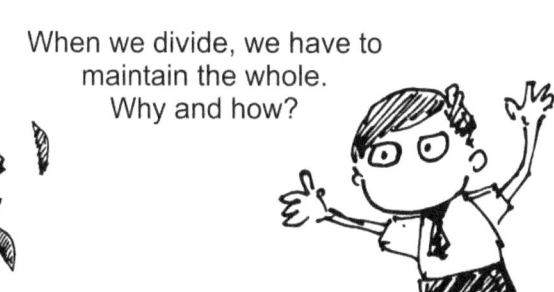

To retain reality? Any reality must be whole.

Complementarity is the way to harmonize an object into a whole.

The Hidden Mysteries of Tao Philosophy

The opposites complement each other to represent a reality.

Then, the two opposites lead to the same result.!

That is true only if we can follow the principle of Tao.

A Sage follows the principle, so he can do either way to achieve the same goal.

By not striving for something, he can strive for anything without any opposition !

So without doing something, he can accomplish that thing.

By dividing, we preserve the whole.
The ancient principle is not just words.

We have to observe the principle!

Chapter 24   Tiptoeing

Our attempt to uphold anything will fragment the whole and often result in failure of that thing because that object has lost its anchor.

For examples, by tiptoeing, one cannot stand firm. By striding, we cannot walk far. If we are assertive to be appreciated, we will not be appreciated. If we want to show ourselves, we will grow dim. If we boast to get merit, we cannot gain merit. If we pride ourselves, we cannot foster others.

This is just the principle of Tao. We do not have to do these extraneous things. They are like tumors on a body or the leftover after a meal. They serve no purpose and should all be avoided. Therefore, anyone with Tao will avoid these.

1　企者不立，跨者不行。
2　自是者不彰，自見者不明，
　　自伐者無功，自矜者不長。
3　其在道也。曰：餘食贅行。物或惡之，
4　故有道者弗居。

The Hidden Mysteries of Tao Philosophy

Tiptoeing cannot stand firm.
Striding cannot walk far.

Anything revealed cannot last.

Explicit act to strive for distinction will not bring lasting distinction.

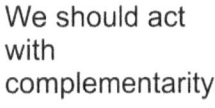

Chapter 25　Unity of All

Nature exists as One before we designate heaven and earth. There is a strong union of man, earth, heaven, and Tao in nature. Nature appears chaotic and we identify the myriad things from this source. We do not know how to describe this order. Lao-tzu calls it Tao.

Tao seems indefinite and infinite. Being infinite, it can sustain, and so it can reach far and can return to repeat itself as One. Tao, heaven and earth are united as One. Their infinite unifying power 王 preserves the Oneness of all.

Therefore, there are four infinities (Tao, heaven, earth, and the unifying power) in nature. Man abides by the earth; the earth abides by heaven; the heaven abides by the Tao. Tao abides by nature. This is the state of Oneness.

1　有物混成，先天地生。
　　寂呵寥呵，獨立而不改，可以為天地母。
2　吾不知其名，字之曰道。吾強為之名曰大。
3　大曰逝，逝曰遠，遠曰返。
　　道大，天大，地大，王亦大。
4　國中有四大，而王居一焉。
5　人法地，地法天，天法道，道法自然。

The Hidden Mysteries of Tao Philosophy

So, there are three entities and one unifying power.

These three are united as One.

Man follows the earth ...

Earth follows heaven ...

Heaven follows Tao.

Tao follows nature. Nature is Onen.

Tao, heaven, and earth are united as One.

Chapter 26   Anchoring

In complementarity, one object serves as an anchor for its opposite. Each object must gain support of its opposite in order to last. For example, anchoring to heaviness and tranquility are important to allow lightness and restlessness to become stable. Each pair forms a pattern of complementarity.

However, this does not mean that heaviness and tranquility are more important than lightness and restlessness. For example, tranquility could also anchor on restlessness. Anchoring is mutual and reciprocal.

There are many examples of anchoring on to a base. However, Lao-tzu does not prefer any one type of object, such as heaviness or tranquility. He just shows the need for complementarity. We are often chasing an object at the expense of its opposite.

If we lose the anchor of an object, the object may become reckless.

1   重為輕根，靜為躁君。
2   是以君子終日行，不離其輜重。雖有營觀，燕居則超若。
3   奈何萬乘之主，而以身輕於天下？
4   輕則失本，躁則失君。

The Hidden Mysteries of Tao Philosophy

For any characteristic to last, that one must be anchored to its opposite.

Lightness will be secured, if it is anchored to something heavy.

Likewise, restlessness must be anchored to tranquility.

A man should not act far from his anchoring principle...

So he can act freely.

A man with splendors remains detached.

Yes. His splendors are anchored on his detachment.

No wonder a mighty lord would discounts his own significance, so his significance can last.

By acting lightly, one will lose one's principle.
By acting restlessly, one will lose one's guidance.

Chapter 27   Without Traces

Within Oneness, there will be no traces of our actions because everything remain in harmony. All actions will be concealed. Oneness state is self-healing.

If we walk according to the principle of Tao, there will be no trace. If we speak according to the principle, there will be no blemish. If we plot according to the principle, there is no sign for any plot.

By the same token, when everything is kept in harmony, there is no way to disturb it. A good lock will not show any latch, so it cannot be opened. A good tie will not show any knot, so it cannot be untied.

A Sage acts with the principle of Tao, so he will not discriminate against anyone or anything. Nothing will be abandoned. A master is our master; a non-master is also a resources for us. If we do not treat all things as useful contributions to the whole, we go astray. This is the essence of the principle of Tao.

1   善行者無轍跡；善言者無瑕謫。善數者不用籌策。
2   善閉者無關鑰 而不可啟也；善結無繩約 而不可解也。
3   是以聖人恆善救人，而無棄人。物無棄材，是謂襲明。
4   故善人，善人之師；不善人，善人 之資也。
5   不貴其師，不愛其資，雖智乎大迷，
6   是謂妙要。

Any action that preserves the whole will leave no trace for itself.

How can we act without leaving any trace?

If the action is harmonious with the environment, everything will remain as One.

If we can maintain Oneness, nothing becomes explicit.
No object will show.

The Hidden Mysteries of Tao Philosophy

The best lock will show no latch... So it cannot be unlocked.

So the best tie shows no knot, so it cannot be untied.

A Sage treats everything without differentiation. He takes care of all.

He is impartial in helping people.

He adheres to the light of Oneness and follow it.

    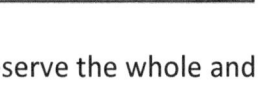

The *Subtle Essence* of Tao is to preserve the whole and treat all objects equally.

Chapter 28   Grand System of Tao

This Chapter discusses the process to establish a system of Tao in the dualistic world. We have to integrate the dualistic objects into a whole.

The sharp and strong characteristics of the objects are transformed with the proper law of interactions (恆德) that will restore Oneness of all. Lao-tzu uses several examples to show how we can return to Infancy, to Simplicity, and to Wu-ji 無極, as the state of Oneness.

This state of Oneness can then disperse to establish the vessels of Tao. A Sage also observes this process to guide the people to build a Grand System of Tao. By observing the principle of Tao, the Grand System will not be fragmented.

1   知其雄，守其雌，為天下谿。為天下谿，恆德不離。
    恆德不離，復歸於嬰兒。
2   知其榮，守其辱，為天下谷。為天下谷，恆德乃足。
    恆德乃足。復歸於樸。
3   知其白，守其黑，為天下式。為天下式，恆德不忒。
    恆德不忒，復歸於無極。
4   樸散則為器。聖人用則為官長。
5   故大制無割。

Interpretations of the Chapters

A Grand System of Tao can be built on our dualistic views, as long as we can harmonize, complement, and reduce all views into One.

Seeking harmony...

Harmonize all opposites into softness and tenderness. Return to the state of an infant.

Accept all opposites with the heart deep as a valley and return to simplicity.

Establishing simplicity...

The Hidden Mysteries of Tao Philosophy

Remove all polarization...

The ultimate state is without polarization. The state of Oneness.

無極

We then have the foundation to build a system of Tao. Oneness can diffuse to form various vessels of Tao.

So everything will adhere to Oneness.

The Sage will use the same principle to guide the people to build a Grand System of Tao in the world.

Then, the system will not be fragmented.

Chapter 29   Controlling Nature

The order of nature should not be perturbed with our actions for our purposes. The world has its own nature. We should let it be. Only some actions may be used to eradicate deviations from this nature, but these actions should only be used reluctantly.

If we try to change the world by our own will, we will induce failure in the system. If we try to alter its course by our own will, it will go astray. The important thing is to let things run their own natural courses.

It is hard to impose our actions on the world in order to improve any part of it. The most important thing is recognize that some will lead and some will follow. Some hush and some shout. Some strong and some weak. Some grow and some fail. This is always parts of nature.

What we need to do is only to eradicate the extremes, the exuberance, and the nonessential extras that fragment the whole. A Sage only abide with Oneness.

1   將欲取天下而為之，吾見其弗得已。
     夫天下神器也，非可為者也。
2   為之者敗之，執之者失之。
3   故物或行或隨；或噓或吹；或強或羸；或培或墮。
4   是以聖人去甚，去泰，去奢。

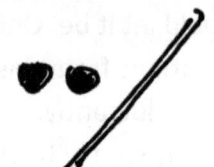

Interpretations of the Chapters

Should we just let the things be?

Yes. Some will lead and some will follow. Everything has its natural part in the whole.

We are just parts of the world.

The Sage only acts to eradicate the extremes, the sparkles, and the nonessentials.

We are still not passive in the world?

We should observe the principle of Tao.

Chapter 30 Wars

Wars are the last resort used to correct deviations from the nature order. The only purpose of a war is to return everything back to harmony. When the correction is achieved, one should just withdraw and remain concealed again. Anything not concealed will decay away.

Lao-tzu is not against or pro war, but he has a principle in carrying out a war. He considers wars a major disruption of our life and nature, and war should be used only as a reluctant action to restore the nature. Once a harmonious condition is achieved, the war effort should stop.

War is not to show strength. Our strength used should not go beyond the desired settlement. Anything continues to show strength will lead to decay and is against Tao. Lao-tzu warns that whatever is against Tao will perish early.

1　以道佐人主，不以兵強於天下。其事好還。
　　師之所居，荊棘生之。
2　善者 果而已矣，毋以取強焉。
　　果而毋驕，果而勿矜，果而勿伐，
3　果而毋得已居，是謂果而不強。
4　物牡而老。是謂之不道，不道早已。

Interpretations of the Chapters

Is a war justified as the last resort eradicate deviations from the nature?

Lao-tzu says that we should not advise a lord to use arms.

When we deploy the troops, we destroy and waste the land.

Wars often invite retaliations, so it becomes endless.

Interpretations of the Chapters

Just to return the world to harmony.	So, the goal of the war is to return back to normality.

Winning is not something to dwell on.	We just return to harmony!	Conceal the strength again?

Showing any strength will lead to decline. It is against Tao!

Whatever is against Tao will perish early.

Chapter 31 War Victory

Lao-tzu regards wars as unfortunate. War should be used only as the last resort. Man of Tao should avoid wars. Even a war victory is treated as something unfortunate. Everyone dislikes wars. Military events are inauspicious.

How do we treat wars as inauspicious events? It can be seen from the victory ceremony. For auspicious events, the honor is designated to the left; but, in funeral services, the honor is designated to the right. The war ceremony follows the arrangement of a funeral service.

The Lieutenant Generals sit on the left-hand side and the Senior Generals sit on the right-hand side. So military victory celebration is treated as a funeral.

Military action should be used with great care, and without glorifying it. In a war, there will be many deaths. This should be remembered with great sorrows.

1　夫兵者，不祥之器，物或惡之，故有道者弗居。
2　君子居則貴左，用兵則貴右。故兵者非君子之器也。
3　兵者不祥之器也，不得已而用之。恬淡為上，勿美也。
4　若美之，是樂殺人也。夫樂殺人，不可以得志於天下矣。
5　是以吉事上左，喪事上右。是以偏將軍居左，上將軍居右。言以喪禮居之也。
6　殺人眾，以悲哀涖之，戰勝而以喪禮處之。

The Hidden Mysteries of Tao Philosophy

To glorify a war is to rejoice in killing people.

Whoever rejoices in killing cannot prevail in the world. That is why a victory ceremony is like a funeral ! Senior Generals are on the right with no honor.

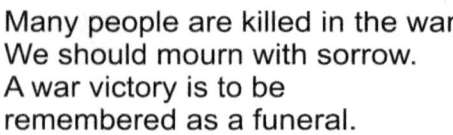

Many people are killed in the war.
We should mourn with sorrow.
A war victory is to be
remembered as a funeral.

Chapter 32   Establishing a System

Tao always remains in the state of Oneness, which may appears insignificant, but cannot be subdued by anyone. If we can follow it, everything will be in harmony. Nature will be self-adjusting.

Lao-tzu describes the state of Oneness as an un-carved wood block (樸), which is characterized as Simplicity because it lacks any recognized feature.

We can slowly form a system of Tao from this state of Oneness by designating various objects and organizations. All objects assume their natural roles in a system of Tao. The process will automatically stop and all objects can remain concealed. Such a process will not lead to any danger.

The way these "parts" contribute to the Grand system of Tao is the same as the way many small streams in the valley contribute to the river and oceans. This system of Tao is built from seemingly insignificant traces of Tao.

1　道恆無名。樸雖小，而天下弗敢臣。
2　侯王若能守之，萬物將自賓。
3　天地相合，以雨甘露，民莫之令而自均焉。
4　始制有名，名亦既有，夫亦將知止，知止所以不殆。
5　譬道之在天下也，猶小谷之與江海也。

The Hidden Mysteries of Tao Philosophy

 Tao is hard to describe since it is or great simplicity.

 However, it cannot be subdued by anyone.

 If a lord can maintain such a state...

 Everything will settle in its proper place.

Heaven and earth will be in harmony and the dews will be sweet. Everything will self-adjust without any further mandate.

Interpretations of the Chapters

With this foundation, we may start to build a system of Tao.

We identify and assign names to the myriad things, with proper boundaries.

How do we maintain the whole?

The process will self-adjust to form the system.

All things silently contribute to the whole system.

It is just like little streams flowing to form the vast rivers and the seas.

Chapter 33 Inner and Outer

We often have multiple manifestations for a reality. For example, one from outside and one from inside. We use external knowledge to know others and use inner insight to see ourselves. We use power to overcome others and use inner strength to overcome ourselves. When the inner strength and external power are equivalent, we have truly achieved Oneness.

Lao-tzu cites the examples of the real wealth is anchored on our inner contentment, and the real persistency is anchored on inner will. Here we have achieved the proper pattern as the complementarity of inner and external objects as a whole. That is in full compliance with the principle of Tao.

One can truly endure long if one can maintain such a state. The true longevity is to die without deviating from the principle of Tao.

1 知人者智也，自知者明也。
   勝人者有力也，自勝者強也。
2 知足者富也。強行者有志也。
3 不失其所者久也。死而不亡者壽也。

Interpretations of the Chapters

Knowing others requires knowledge. That is external.

Knowing oneself requires insight. That is internal.

Overcoming others requires power. That is external.

Overcoming oneself requires strength.

That is internal!

In true harmony, both inner and outer qualities are important and should be reconciled as One.

That is the true integrated state of Oneness.

| Wealth and contentment are reconciled.. | Will and persistence are reconciled. | The external and the inner are integrated! |

So we can truly return to the state of Oneness!

Only with Oneness, it can be everlasting.

That is the ultimate proper state!

Those staying in the proper state will endure long;
Those perishing without deviating from Oneness have true longevity.

Chapter 34   Tao Floods

Tao prevails allover and nothing can escape from it. It performs all tasks without showing itself.

Tao never acts as a lord. When accepting the myriad things without discrimination, it appears to act small. When the myriad things return to it, it appears to act big. Tao can achieve both big and small tasks with the same action.

Actually, both acts lead to the same goal. Even the act is small, a great task is accomplished. By the same principle, even if the Sage acts small, the result of its opposite (acting big) is accomplished.[13]

This is the way a Sage can accomplish his (own) great goals by not acting with great importance.

1　大道氾呵，其可左右也。
　　成功遂事而弗名有也。
2　萬物歸焉而弗為主，則恆無欲，可名於小。
3　萬物歸焉而弗為主，可名於大。
4　是以聖人之能成大也，以其不為大也，故能成大。

---

[13] See Introduction for more discussion on this usual logical conclusion.

Tao is so vast. It floods all overall, but it accomplishes its tasks without showing itself.

It acts as though it is nothing.

Sometimes, it acts big and sometimes, it acts small.

You are dualistic again! It acts big and small at the same time.

When all things turn to it, it receives all without acting as a lord and it appears humble and small.

At the same time, it is where all things return to. It accept all as a great lord.

Interpretations of the Chapters

 So Tao can act small and big at the same time.

 The two opposites lead to the same goal.

 If acting according to Tao, a Sage can accomplish great tasks without acting great.

The same result may be achieved in both ways. The key is to follow the principle of Tao carefully.

 That is so true.

Chapter 35   Great Image

Tao is like a big sign for the world to follow. If we just follow the sign, we will have peace and safety. Everything moves toward it without any hindrance. Tao is silent and bland, but it still attracts us to stop by and follow it.

Although Tao is invisible and inaudible, its function is inexhaustible.

1   執大象，天下往。往而不害，安平太。
2   樂與餌，過客止。
3   故道之出言也，曰淡乎其無味也。
4   視之不足見也，聽之不足聞也，用之不可既也。

 Tao is like a Great Image upheld high that the whole world can follow.

There will be no hindrance and the world will rest in peace and prosperity.

Why are we attracted to Tao?

Normally we are attracted by music or baits.

But, Tao is bland and tasteless.
We really do not know why
we are attracted to Tao.

We cannot see it.
We cannot hear it.

However, it has been so useful and
its function cannot be
exhausted!

Chapter 36   On Shrinking

To properly describe a phenomenon, two opposite actions must happen simultaneously.

This is difficult to perceive because we misplace our discussions on the actions instead of the phenomenon. In any phenomenon, both actions must simultaneously be initiated. This is a very *Delicate Insight* (微明) in Tao philosophy.

Therefore, shrinking and expansion must occur as a pattern, not as two independent events. As objects, shrinking and expanding are rigid and strong but the actualities are "soft and weak." Lao-tzu clearly prefer "soft and weak" over "rigid and strong."

When a thing is separated out of the whole, the thing cannot last. That is why a fish cannot be separated from the stream and weapons of a state should not be disclosed.

1　將欲翕之，必固張之；將欲弱之，必固強之；
　　將欲去之，必固舉之；將欲奪之，必固予之。
　　是謂微明。
2　柔弱勝強。
3　魚不可脫於淵，國利器不可以示人。

We use two things to describe a phenomenon.
When we describe the phenomenon,
These two things must happen at the same time.

The two things form a pattern of complementarity.

The phenomenon is shrinking and expanding.

In reality, both events are there in complementarity. Therefore, shrinking must also contain expanding.

How can you see expansion when it is shrinking?

We have to think of reality, not the dualistic objects.

Interpretations of the Chapters

Chapter 37   Self-Rectifying

As stated in Chapter 32, we should let everything evolve within the state of Oneness (Pu 樸), in which everything is harmonized.

Tao cannot be clearly described but everything emerges from this order. If the lord can maintain this order, the myriad things will evolve or transform naturally. The world will be self-rectifying and self-making.

When the myriad things start to form in the state of Oneness, the formation process observes the state of Oneness. In this state, the myriad things will remain concealed and stay in tranquility. The world can then be self-rectified.

1   道恆無名。侯王若能守之，萬物將自化。
2   化而欲作，吾將鎮之以無名之樸。
3   鎮之以無名之樸，夫將不欲。
4   不欲以靜，天下將自正。

Chapter 38   The Hierarchy

Lao-tzu identifies a hierarchy in Tao philosophy. At each level, the principle of Tao remains applicable.

When we are in harmony with Tao, Te is implicit. When we have lost harmony with Tao, Te becomes explicit as the rules of actions. We may identify acting with implicit Te is called Wu-wei 無為 and acting with explicit Te is called Yu-wei 有為. There is a demarcation.

In the highest level, we can act with Wu-wei when we are in harmony with Tao, where all things are concealed. In the next level of Ren 仁, we can still act with Wu-wei because all things are treated equal and Te is still implicit. In the next level of Yi 義, we have to discriminate against different objects so we act with Yu-wei.

In the lowest level of Li 禮, we act with rituals. If we do not get proper response, we get anxious. We are on the verge of disorder. Therefore, we all strive to be at the higher levels.

1 上德不德，是以有德；下德不失德，是以無德。
2 上德無爲而無以爲也；上仁爲之而無以爲也；上義爲之而有以爲也。上禮爲之而莫之應也，則攘臂而扔之。
3 故失道而後德，失德而後仁，失仁而後義，失義而後禮。
4 夫禮者，忠信之薄也，而亂之首也。
  前識者，道之華也，而愚之首也。
5 是以大丈夫居其厚而不居其薄，居其實而不居其華。
6 故去彼取此。

Interpretations of the Chapters

The Hidden Mysteries of Tao Philosophy

Rituals are the ornaments of Tao. Relying on rituals is a sign of ignorance.

What should we do?

Rules often become superficial.

We should go back to the principle of Tao and seek the essence of Tao.

We should choose essence and avoid ornaments.

Chapter 39   Maintaining Oneness

Heaven attains Oneness to have clarity, but it cannot always be clear. If it stays clear all the time, it will fragment Oneness. The earth attains Oneness to have tranquility. But it cannot be always tranquil.

There are many examples, such as omnipotence of gods, abundance of the spirit, and the rectification power of a lord. Their Oneness is inclusive of all states. Striving to reveal any state exclusively will end up with nothing.

We should not have anything sparkling like jades or clattering like stones. These things have overflown from the concealment.

1   昔之得一者：天得一以清，地得一以寧，
     神得一以靈，谷得一以盈，侯王得一以為天下正。
2   其致之也。謂天毋已清，將恐裂；地毋已寧，將恐廢；
     神毋已靈，將恐歇；谷毋已盈，將恐竭；
     侯王毋已貴以高，將恐蹶。
3   故必貴而以賤為本，必高矣而以下為基。
     夫是以侯王自謂孤、寡、不穀。此其賤之本，與非也？
4   故致數譽無譽。
5   是故不欲琭琭若玉，珞珞若石。

Interpretations of the Chapters

A lord anchor his high status on his lowly names, so his status can last.

He calls himself: a widower, a worthless, etc.

For anything to last, it must be anchored on or complemented by its opposite, in order to become whole.

If we strive for dignity alone, we will end up without any dignity!

For anything to last forever, it must be concealed.

We should avoid sparkling like jades, or clattering like stones.

Chapter 40   Dynamics of Tao

This short Chapter summarizes the principle of Tao philosophy. We think in dualism. The dynamics of Tao is to include both opposites into realities. The function of Tao is to soften the objects in realities.

By including the opposite, the rigid and strong characteristics of the objects are harmonized and the patterns are tender and soft.

When we characterize the myriad things by their sameness or difference, as Lao-tzu has done in Chapter 1, the dynamics of Tao shows that the myriad things are always formed simultaneously by Wu and Yu, as two opposite objects in complementarity. This Chapter is a natural conclusion of the complementarity discussed in Chapter 1.

1　反也者道之動也；弱也者道之用也。
2　天下之物生於有，生於無。

Interpretations of the Chapters

The dynamic of Tao is to invoke the opposite to maintain the whole.

The function of Tao is to soften the objects by concealing the objects

The myriad things are formed due to the differences in nature.

The myriad things are also formed due to the sameness in nature.

Everything shows sameness and differences!

All opposites must be in complementarity.

Concluding Remarks

We have summarized the basic features of the logic of Tao philosophy in the Introduction. These principles appear repeatedly in many chapters of the *Tao Te Ching*. The main characteristics is the complementarity of dualistic objects. For a full description of the Logic of Tao Philosophy, readers should refer to detailed formulation in other volumes in the *Series*.

We have chosen to publish this volume by including the first forty chapters of the *Tao Te Ching* as examples. This volume will be expanded to include the rest of the *Tao Te Ching* in the future.

The main concepts of the logic of Tao philosophy are now well-founded, but some details are still evolving.

We have used the Print-on-Demand technology to publish all the books in the *Searching for Tao Series* so the contents of all related books are constantly updated. We try our best to keep the updates on the same pace.

ABOUT THE AUTHORS

Wayne L. Wang has been an independent researcher on Tao philosophy since 1999. He became interested in Tao philosophy because the *Tao Te Ching* has been treated as a mysterious philosophy, but shows some similarities to scientific phenomena.

He has devoted his time in further clarification of the principle of Tao philosophy. He has published The Basic Theory of Tao Philosophy (2006), which shows an initial scientific model reflecting the Tai-ji relationship in Tao. He first published a complete logic structure in a Chinese article *The Logic of Tao Philosophy* (2012). The model and its application are summarized in two books: *The Logic of Tao Philosophy* (2013) and *Tao Te Ching: An Ultimate Translation* (2013). His recent work is about *Systems Thinking and Logic of Tao Philosophy* (2016).

These works represent a major milestone in his search for the foundation of Tao philosophy. This makes a logical and self-consistent translation of the *Tao Te Ching* possible. He holds a Ph. D. degree from M. I. T. and resides near Chicago, Illinois, USA. Please send your comments and suggestions to:

    email: wwwang@alum.mit.edu.

    Website: http://www.dynamictao.wordpress.com/

Lekki Chua, born in 1936, a Taiwanese American. Lekki is most known for the uncanny life like qualities of his portraits, and the expressive use of light in the still life. His keen manipulation light and color is no surprise, given his professional background in graphic design and photography. Lekki's artistic career began early and has taken many manifestations. Even as child he knew he wanted to be an artist, and his first job was as an illustrator for a children's magazine.

He has painted throughout his whole life and now that he is retired, can devote more time to the serious pursuit of his artistic goals, an undertaking he regards as his second career. Primarily self-taught, many still consider his early watercolors to be among his best work. 1999 Lekki joined the Palette and Chisel at Chicago, and 2001 began to taking class at College Of DuPage.

He has always admired the impressionist, but is working diligently to find and refine a style of his own. Most of his work can be considered 'realism', with recent forays into expressionism. No longer content to merely 'copy the form', he is intent on giving representation to his Visio, and finding the way distill and impart of his 60 or so years of experience, "I can capture the shape of something very easily-it is my gift. But it doesn't express my own fillings, so I am trying to spend more time to capture the color and my own opinions about the subject". Attaining this goal would meet Lekki's own definition of a 'real artist', and fulfill his wish of a lifetime.

Lekki paints under his childhood nickname "Lekki" and lives in Roselle Illinois with his wife Mei.

www.ingramcontent.com/pod-product-compliance
Lightning Source LLC
Chambersburg PA
CBHW061650040426
42446CB00010B/1675